Daniela De Luca

It's a WILDLIFE, Buddy!

Celia
the Tiger

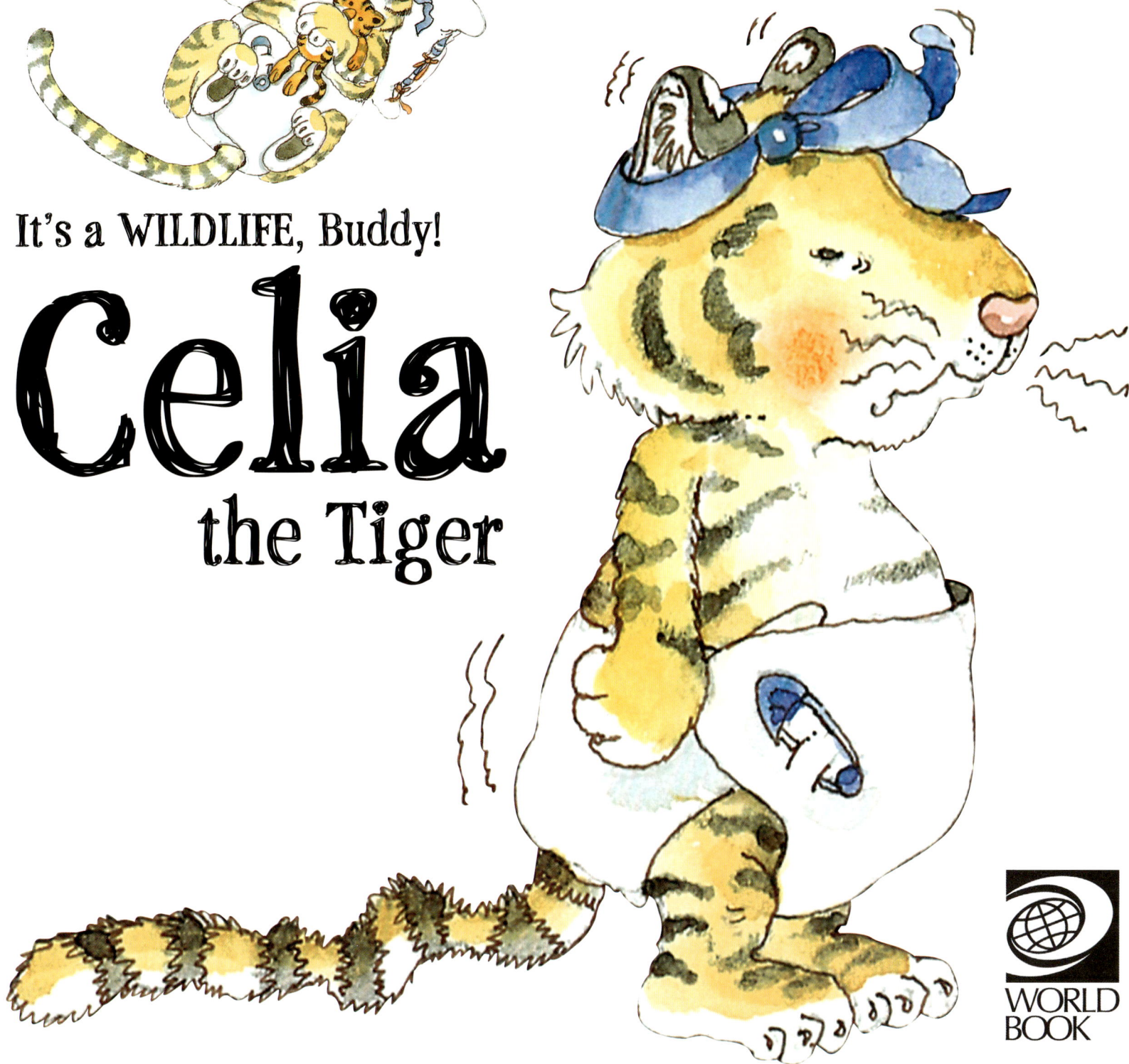

WORLD BOOK

World Book, Inc.
180 North LaSalle Street
Suite 900
Chicago, Illinois 60601
USA

For school and library sales, please phone
1-800-975-3250 (United States)
or 1-800-837-5365 (Canada).

www.worldbook.com

LIBRARY OF CONGRESS
CATALOGING-IN-PUBLICATION DATA
HAS BEEN APPLIED FOR.

Copyright © 2017 by Nextquisite Ltd, London
Publishers: Anne McRae, Marco Nardi
www.nextquisite.com

All illustrations by Daniela De Luca
Texts: Daniela De Luca, Anne McRae, Neil Morris
Editing: Anne McRae, Vicky Egan, Neil Morris
Graphic Design: Marco Nardi
Layout: Marco Nardi, Rebecca Milner

This edition edited and revised by World Book, Inc.
by permission of Nextquisite Ltd.

ISBN: 978-0-7166-3519-2 (set), 978-0-7166-3524-6 (Celia the Tiger)

Printed and bound in China
1st printing March 2017

As soon as Celia is born, deep in the jungle in the heart of India, her mother realizes that this tiger cub is a little different. Young Celia likes to suck her tail and hug her teddy cat. In fact, she acts more like a scared kitten than the daughter of a fearless jungle queen.

HOW DOES A MOTHER TIGER LOOK AFTER HER CUBS?

A mother tiger's two or three cubs are born blind. She carries them gently in her mouth. They start going for short walks with her when they are about four months old. By their first birthday they can hunt for themselves. And when they are two years old they are ready to leave their mother to go off on their own.

HOW DOES A TIGER HUNT?

First, the tiger sees its prey, that is, the animal it wants to hunt.

Then the tiger hides in the tall grass ...

MOTHER TIGER DECIDES NOT TO WORRY that Celia is such a scaredy-cat. She'll soon learn, Mother thinks, when I show her how to hunt. "First you must look for your prey," she tells Celia firmly.

6

... and suddenly **pounces**!

The tiger kills its prey using its sharp claws and teeth.

CELIA SPOTS SOME PREY in a nearby bush. But it gives her an awful fright. "Whatever can it be?" wonders Mother, as Celia jumps into her arms.

Goodness! It's just a little mouse that has frightened Celia. "Let's leave the hunting for now," sighs Mother.

HOW BIG ARE TIGERS?

Siberian tigers are the biggest. Adult males grow up to nearly 11 feet (3.3 m) long and can weigh as much as 700 pounds (320 kilograms). Females are a bit smaller.

DO TIGERS LIKE TO KEEP CLEAN?

Yes. Tigers spend up to 20 hours a day resting, and for part of this time they lick their fur to keep it clean.

NEXT, MOTHER DECIDES to give Celia a swimming lesson. But this doesn't go well either. Unlike all her tiger cousins, Celia is afraid of the water!

10

DO TIGERS REALLY LIKE WATER?

Yes, unlike many other cats, they do! When it gets very hot, they like to lie in a stream or pool to cool down. They are good swimmers, too.

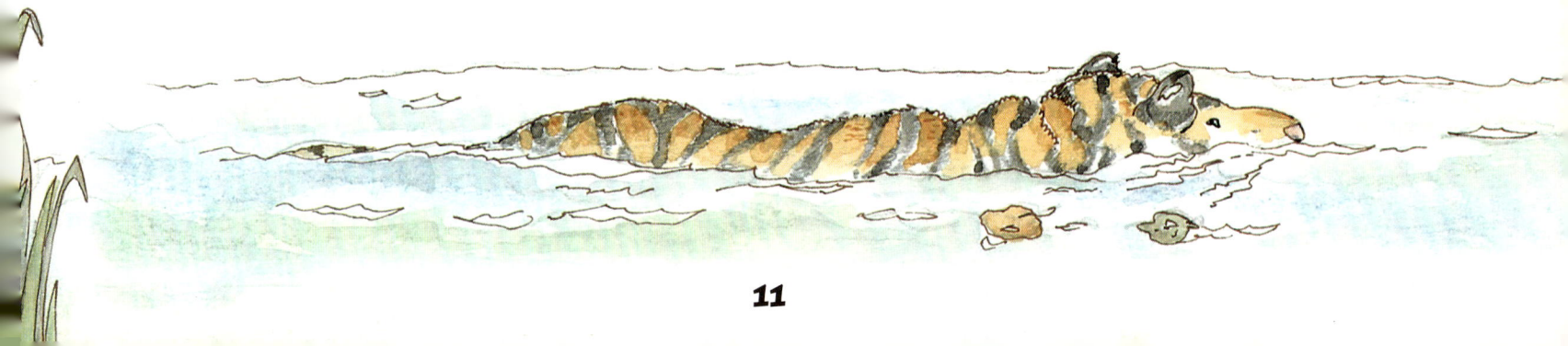

MOTHER TIGER BEGINS to realize that
she needs help if she is ever to help
Celia be fearless. So she invites all her
friends for a cup of tea and a chat. When
the jungle animals hear about the problem,
they look doubtful and shake their heads.
"You'd better ask the Old Wise One for
advice," they suggest.

12

BRIAN SLOTH BEAR

MRS. PRIYA
ASIAN ELEPHANT

DAKSH
COBRA

AARON TREE SHREW

JOHN HOG BADGER

13

MR. AND
MRS. CHITAL
SPOTTED DEER,
WITH BRITA AND
SHIBHI

PRAJEET BLACK
LEOPARD

BHARAT CRANE

MOTHER TIGER

ABIGAIL INDIAN
RHINOCEROS

CELIA

JEEVAN
MONGOOSE

BALRAM AND MADHU MACAQUE

14

WHAT DO TIGERS EAT?

Mostly they eat large animals, such as wild buffalo, pigs, antelope, and deer. But sometimes they catch smaller prey, too, such as monkeys, squirrels, and prickly porcupines. When they want just a snack, they might even catch fish, frogs, crabs, lizards, or snakes.

DEER

FROG

WILD BUFFALO

WARTHOG

RED SQUIRREL

MOTHER TIGER AND CELIA climb to the top of a high rock. From there they can see the place where the Old Wise One lives.

ARE SOME TIGERS WHITE?

Once in a long while an orange mother tiger has a white cub. White tigers have blue eyes, pink noses, and brown stripes. Some even have no stripes at all. In India, only about twelve white tigers have been seen in the last 100 years.

16

HOW MANY KINDS OF TIGER ARE THERE?

There are only six subspecies, or kinds, of tiger still alive in the wild: the Bengal, Indochinese, Siberian, South China, Malayan, and Sumatran. Even these tigers are in danger of dying out, and many people work hard to protect them.

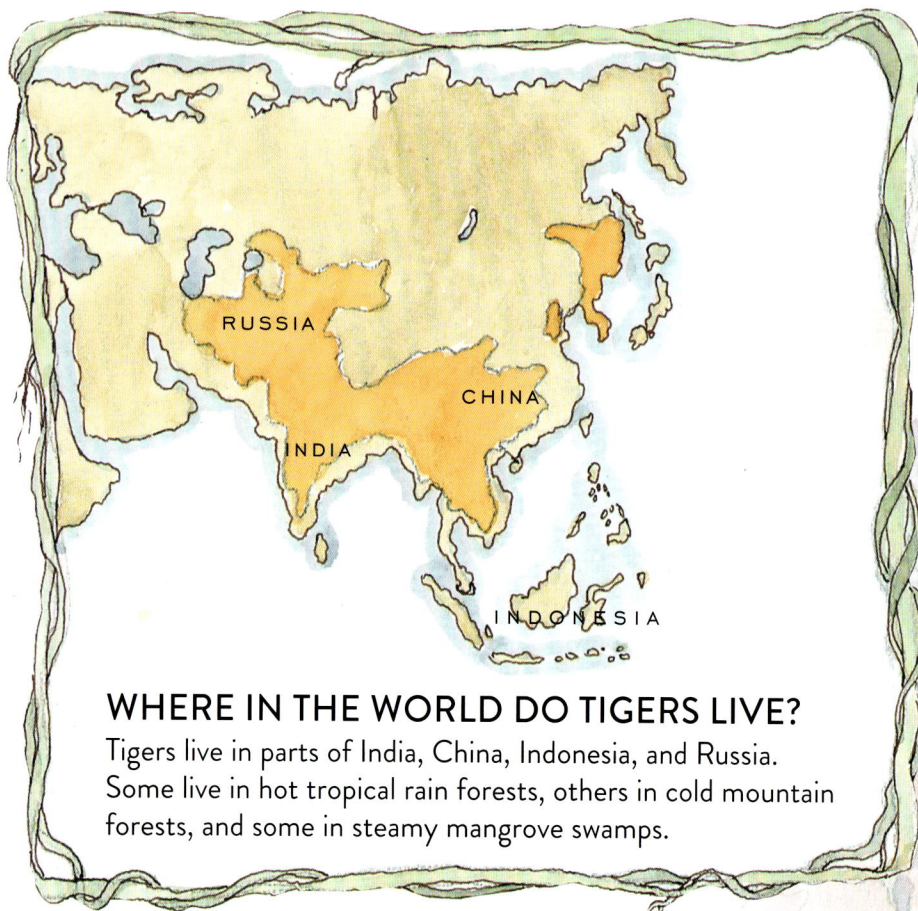

WHERE IN THE WORLD DO TIGERS LIVE?

Tigers live in parts of India, China, Indonesia, and Russia. Some live in hot tropical rain forests, others in cold mountain forests, and some in steamy mangrove swamps.

IT IS NEARLY SUNSET by the time they reach the monkey temple. The Old Wise One listens to Mother Tiger and then gives her advice. "All will be well when the cub makes a friend," she says wisely.

NEXT MORNING, Mother Tiger goes off early to hunt for breakfast. When Celia wakes up to find she is all alone, she jumps out of bed and rushes off to find her mother.

But Celia has a nasty surprise
when she falls straight into a hole!

It's NOT just any old hole. It's a trap made by human hunters. The hunters hope to catch jungle animals in their trap.

Now Celia is well and truly stuck!
Luckily, Rhino, the baby rhinoceros,
sees what happened. But can he help?

RHINO FINDS A ROPE and uses all
his strength to pull Celia out of
the hole.

Then together they wait for
Mother Tiger to come back
from hunting.

24

LATER THAT DAY, Mother says Celia can go and play with Rhino. Both young animals are happy and have fun together in the jungle.

HOW DO TIGERS KEEP THEIR CLAWS SHARP?

They scratch tree trunks! When they walk, they pull their claws into their toes so the claws don't wear down.

In fact, Celia is so busy having fun that—almost without realizing it—she soon learns how to hunt and swim. With Rhino around, she's not scared any more.

WHY DO TIGERS HAVE STRIPES?

So they can hide in tall grass when they are hunting. The **camouflage** helps to break up their shape. No two tigers have the same pattern of stripes!

MOTHER TIGER watches contentedly
as Celia and Rhino play together.
The Old Wise One was right about friends.
And now Celia plays some very daring games
as tigers ought to do!

WILDCAT

GEOFFROY'S CAT

GOLDEN CAT

MOUNTAIN LION

DID YOU KNOW?

All cats, both big and small, belong to one animal family. Most cats—except lions—like to hunt on their own at night. The main difference between big cats, like tigers and lions, and small cats, such as our pet cats, is that the little ones can purr, and the big ones can roar.

LYNX

(ANIMALS ARE NOT SHOWN TO SCALE.)

LION

OCELOT

CHEETAH

The big cats are strong and fierce. But they and other large wild animals need help from people to have enough space to live and find food and be kept safe from hunters.

LEOPARD

CELIA

PALM CIVET

FLYING
SQUIRREL

Here is Celia with her many
new friends. They all live in
Asia. How many have you
learned about?

GAUR

CHITAL
(AXIS DEER)

SUN BEAR

INDIAN RHINOCEROS

TARSIER

TAPIR

GIANT PANDA

ORANGUTAN

HIMALAYAN TAHR

LIZARD

SHREW

30

(ANIMALS ARE NOT SHOWN TO SCALE.)

GIBBON

PEACOCK

BAT

BACTRIAN CAMEL

ASIAN ELEPHANT

PYTHON

SARUS CRANE

BLACK LEOPARD

COBRA

MONGOOSE

CELIA

HAMSTER

MONITOR LIZARD

31

Glossary

Terms defined in this glossary are in type that **looks like this** (bold type) on their first appearance on any two facing pages (a spread).

advice - helpful information; a suggestion; guidance

camouflage - something, such as striped fur, that makes it hard for an animal to be seen

pounce - to jump suddenly to catch something

Note to the Grown-Ups: Each "It's a Wildlife, Buddy!" book combines a whimsical narrative and factual background information to help children learn a little life lesson and a few things about some animals with which we share the world. We have the animal characters say and do things that are not possible for them in the wild to create stories that can appeal to children and that they can relate to. The stories can help children think about making friends, growing up, and other important parts of their lives. The fanciful stories are balanced by basic facts about the animals' lives and behaviors in nature. This combination creates a satisfying and informing reading experience whether an adult is reading to a child or a child is reading on his or her own.